COMMUNITY HELPERS

Cashiers

by Kate Moening

BELLWETHER MEDIA • MINNEAPOLIS, MN

Blastoff! Readers are carefully developed by literacy experts to build reading stamina and move students toward fluency by combining standards-based content with developmentally appropriate text.

Level 1 provides the most support through repetition of high-frequency words, light text, predictable sentence patterns, and strong visual support.

Level 2 offers early readers a bit more challenge through varied sentences, increased text load, and text-supportive special features.

Level 3 advances early-fluent readers toward fluency through increased text load, less reliance on photos, advancing concepts, longer sentences, and more complex special features.

★ **Blastoff! Universe**

Reading Level

BLASTOFF! Beginners — Grade **K**

BLASTOFF! READERS — Grades **1–3**

BLASTOFF! DISCOVERY — Grade **4**

This edition first published in 2021 by Bellwether Media, Inc.

No part of this publication may be reproduced in whole or in part without written permission of the publisher. For information regarding permission, write to Bellwether Media, Inc., Attention: Permissions Department, 6012 Blue Circle Drive, Minnetonka, MN 55343.

Library of Congress Cataloging-in-Publication Data

Names: Moening, Kate, author.
Title: Cashiers / by Kate Moening.
Description: Minneapolis, MN : Bellwether Media, Inc., 2021. | Series: Blastoff! Readers: Community helpers | Includes bibliographical references and index. | Audience: Ages 5-8 | Audience: Grades K-1 | Summary: "Developed by literacy experts for students in kindergarten through grade three, this book introduces cashiers to young readers through leveled text and related photos"–Provided by publisher.
Identifiers: LCCN 2020029191 (print) | LCCN 2020029192 (ebook) | ISBN 9781644873991 (library binding) | ISBN 9781648342394 (paperback) | ISBN 9781648340765 (ebook)
Subjects: LCSH: Cashiers–Juvenile literature. | Grocery trade–Juvenile literature. | Occupations–Juvenile literature.
Classification: LCC HF5469 .M64 2021 (print) | LCC HF5469 (ebook) | DDC 51.3/7–dc23
LC record available at https://lccn.loc.gov/2020029191
LC ebook record available at https://lccn.loc.gov/2020029192

Editor: Betsy Rathburn   Designer: Laura Sowers

Printed in the United States of America, North Mankato, MN.

Table of Contents

Shopping Day

The shopper has a full basket. The cashier **scans** the food. Beep!

Next, the shopper pays the cashier. All checked out!

What Are Cashiers?

Cashiers help people buy things. They take payments. They give **change**.

Most cashiers work in stores. Others work in **cafes**!

cafe

What Do Cashiers Do?

Cashiers greet **customers**. They ring up goods with **cash registers**.

cash register

Store cashiers put goods in bags. They give shoppers **receipts**.

receipt

What Makes a Good Cashier?

Cashiers are good at math. They count money.

Cashier Gear

scanner   cash register   bags   receipt

These helpers stand for many hours. They are strong!

Cashier Skills

✓ good with people   ✓ strong

✓ good communicators   ✓ good at math

Cashiers are friendly. They help many customers each day. Cashiers help businesses run!

Glossary

cafes

small restaurants with simple meals and drinks

customers

people who pay for goods or services

cash registers

machines that hold money and say how much a sale costs

receipts

papers that list the cost of each thing that was bought and the total amount paid

change

the money returned when a payment is more than the amount needed

scans

uses a special machine to copy information into a computer

To Learn More

AT THE LIBRARY

Downs, Kieran. *Servers.* Minneapolis, Minn.: Bellwether Media, 2021.

McAnulty, Stacy. *Max Explains Everything: Grocery Store Expert.* New York, N.Y.: G.P. Putnam's Sons, 2018.

Rice, Dona Herweck. *Store Map.* Huntington Beach, Calif.: Teacher Created Materials, 2019.

ON THE WEB

FACTSURFER

Factsurfer.com gives you a safe, fun way to find more information.

1. Go to www.factsurfer.com.

2. Enter "cashiers" into the search box and click Q.

3. Select your book cover to see a list of related content.

Index